Service quality from the guest´s view

AF140100

Frank Höchsmann

Service quality from the guest´s view

Bibliografische Informationen der Deutschen Nationalbibliothek:

Die Deutsche Nationalbibliothek verzeichnet diese Publikation in der Deutschen Nationalbibliographie, detaillierte bibliografische Daten sind im Internet über http: //dnb.dnb.de abrufbar.

Herstellung und Verlag:

BoD – Books on Demand, Norderstedt

ISBN: 9783734735370

Übersetzung: Susanne Höchsmann (Berlin), Katherine Höchsmann (Ottawa)
Revision: Dr. Elisabeth Strecker (Neuenhagen bei Berlin)
Formatierung: Christiane Kretschmer (Fuldatal)
Titel Foto: © Robert Kneschke - Fotolia.com

Autoren Foto: © Frank Höchsmann

Dear reader

Dear participants of seminars

You have chosen one of the most interesting topics.

Congratulations!

Since the beginning of the century we have conducted our courses over 60 times with almost 500 participants from over 20 countries of the world. Therefore, we can proudly say, we have performed in three languages.

The seminar has evolved to "Service quality from the guest´s view" from "Quality in the Hotel-Sector" or "Service-Quality in the Gastronomy-Sector". These were focused on the hardware of the sectors, such as the building itself, furniture, elevators, and so on.

The transition from the focus on quality to the focus on service quality took place on our part already in the year 2000.

Soft-skills, like cordiality, friendliness, honesty and others are now our main point of attention. Implementing these soft-skills leads to customer satisfaction and retention.

The only thing important is what the guest expects, desires and conveys. This is why we always consider the guest´s view.

I hope you enjoy interesting and creative moments with this copy of „Service quality from the guest´s view".

Frank Höchsmann
Berlin, 16.08.2014

Service quality from the guest´s view

Preface

Competition has increased dramatically in the hotel- and gastronomy sector. In addition to that, the expectations, wishes and demands of potential guests have changed substantially. So we have to take these factors in consideration as quality requirements, in order to compete in the market.

Our here described concept depicts international and regional trends, describes what an offer should like and the most important elements in quality and service quality from the view point of the guest. It also includes detailed checklists with over one hundred criteria for quality, in order to implement service quality into day-to-day work.

Our checklists have been proved successfully in several workshops and mystery tests. They have been useful in both, hotel chains and medium-sized hotels and restaurants.

Our checklists are being updated constantly, due to the continuous changes in guests´ expectations. This way the innovative hoteliers and restaurant-owners who implement our concept can and will have an effective system for quality measurement and control at their disposal.

We also provide questionnaires to be filled in by the guests, as to enhance hoteliers and restaurant owners to measure service-quality in a quick manner from the view of the guest. The questionnaires contain ten questions with ten different evaluation options, which have been adopted by hotels top of their class.

Objective

What this well-reviewed concept aims at, is to be able to understand service-quality from the guest´ view and thus to act customer-oriented. We have to ask ourselves the following questions: What is the modern and informed guest expecting? What perception does the guest have from our facility? How can we surpass the expectations? In order to answer these questions hoteliers and restaurant owners have to slip into the guest´s shoes.

Target group

Our target group for the workshops and reference book is hotel and gastronomy staff, how have direct contact to guests.
The topics of this book have been constantly updated with the help of feedback from previous participants of our seminars.

Trends in the hotel and restaurant business

International trends in hotel business

- Increase in number of themed hotels, fun hotels
- Online reviews and bookings
- Conventions and conferences in hotels
- Quality oriented guests
- Environmentally conscious guests
- Issue of loyalty cards or guest discounts (VIP cards)
- Investment of tour operators in hotel chains
- Mergers of independent hotels to co-operations
- Expansion of hotel chains
- Hotel rooms with High-Tech Centres
- International quality-management systems
- Mega-hotels (over 750 rooms)
- Constant staff training

Regional trends in the hotel industry

- New target group: 50+ best agers?
- Increase in business trips, short getaways and culture trips
- Dumping pricing of first-class-hotels on the weekends
- Expansion of co-operations and international hotel chains
- Extremely quality-oriented guests
- Holiday hotels struggle for survival
- Hotel boom in metropolises
- Improvements in quality through renovations, refurbishments and expansion of services
- All inclusive/ complete service

- Increase in conventions and seminars held at hotels
- Increase in environmentally-conscious guests
- Themed hotels rather than just a room to sleep in

Trends in restaurants

- Extremely quality-oriented guests
- Increase in environmentally conscious guests
- Organic food and products
- Convenience food
- Expansion of Asian cuisine and chain restaurants
- Finger food and tapas
- Vegetarian food
- High-Tech Kitchen
- Innovative regional cuisine
- International quality management systems
- Constant staff training
- Restaurant inside restaurant and specialty restaurants
- Issue of loyalty cards or guest discounts (VIP Cards)
- Mergers of independent restaurants to co-operations

Characteristics of the Hotel and Restaurant offerings

- Are composed of material and immaterial components, from hard- and software.
- Hotel offerings are non-storable, so rooms that are not booked are wasted.
- As guests and customers have to go the hotel or restaurant to obtain the service, they are going to the place of service.
- External factors cannot be influenced, e.g. construction disturbing the hotel rooms´ view or any strikes.
- They are substitutable goods, other hotels or restaurants may have similar offerings for a lower price.
- They consist of factors that complement each other, such as transport, accommodation, catering and/or tourist attractions.
- They are difficult to evaluate, as people have different expectations and wishes (the mattress can be too soft for a person, but too hard for another, while being perfect for the third one).
- They are sold before providing the service.
- They depend on the seasons for holiday and beachside hotels.

Components of quality

The following criteria are considered by the guest when evaluating the service quality. This is independent of the price range of the hotel or restaurant.

- Service
- Value-for-money ratio
- Offering (accommodation and/or catering)
- Atmosphere

Expectations, experiences and needs play an important role. If these criteria match the expectations, you have managed to please your guest. Previous studies have shown that service is the most important component of quality.

It is important to remember that a satisfied guest will spread the word about four times, whereas an unsatisfied guest will spread it 16 times. If the guest is not impressed by the service, because it was mediocre, she/he will not talk about it at all or very rarely.

These are the descriptions of the main factors that influence quality:

Service

This is the most important element of quality. You could say it is the key to your success. It is what guest care is all about.

Service is an element that is difficult to measure and consists of two components: The service components and the service performance (depending extremely on the staff).

- Service components: information, reservations, check-in, guest care/ relation, check-out
- Service performance: positive attitude, body language, attentiveness, complaint-management.

Value for money

Due to the growing market transparency and creasing information asymmetries, guests know what to expect for their money. This means that hotels and restaurants have to offer a balanced value-for-money ratio.

Offering

High quality offerings in the hotel sector mean a good quality in terms of space, whereas for restaurants it means a good quality of offered dishes and beverages.

Thus, a hotel should offer a proper ratio of open space to the total area of the room. Furniture has to be classy, depending on the category. Obviously the bed is the main point of attraction in a hotel room.

A restaurant should offer a dish composed of high quality green ware, a professional preparation, complementary side-dishes, spices, adequate quantities, taste, smell and the overall arrangement of the dish.

Atmosphere

Like services, the atmosphere is difficult to measure. It consists of the style of the interior, furniture, decoration, colours, music, temperature, lighting and the odour. Other factors are the accompanying people and neighbours, which are external factors.

So let´s not forget: satisfied guests and customers spread the word four times, whereas unsatisfied guests and customers spread the word 16 times.

It´s the bad truth!

Positive experience   =   4 x

Negative experience = 16 x

Service quality from the hotel guest´s view

This section describes the process of guest care and related services. Following each brief description of best practices, a list of frequently made mistakes and the guest´s expectations follow.

01. First contact

The first contact with the hotel is decisive and will leave lasting impressions, which will be hard to change. This contact has the form of a phone call, the hotel´s website or an agency inquiry.

In case of a call, the guest is expecting the phone to be answered quickly and friendly in their language (answer includes: Name of the hotel and person answering, greeting, a thank you and a short introductory question). The person answering will listen to the guest´s needs and then answer, instead of shooting with information. Because business travellers usually are in a hurry and want to get precise information, whereas tourists usually have more time.

The guest expects a website loading in seven seconds or less and they want it to be clearly structured. The guest should be able to return to the home page from every page of the website. Moreover will a well-structured booking form on the website provide for the booking process of the guest.

Another way of having a first contact with the hotel is via travel agencies or other. Either through a brochure at the agency, or through the agent who informs the clients about the hotel.

The effect of a first contact is often underestimated, which is a big mistake!

Frequent mistakes:

- Answering machine
- Holding the line
- Let the phone ring more than five times
- Technical language/ hotel vocabulary
- Uninformed beginners on the line
- Unfriendly staff on the line
- Too much unnecessary information on websites and in advertising material

Key to success:

- Answering the phone at the third ring at the latest
- Friendly and appropriate welcome
- Quickly loading and well-structured website
- Eye catching advertising material , to attract potential guest´s interest

02. Reservations

In order to professionalize the whole reservation process, the guests should be addressed by their names and the offered room have to comply one hundred percent with the guests' expressed wishes and needs.

If the desired room is not available, two alternatives have to be offered by explaining the differences to the room expected by the guest.

The guest´s personal information will be handled with care and a written confirmation will be offered to the guest. This will be confirmed orally before hanging up the phone:

- Name of the guest
- Arrival and departure dates
- Room type
- Number of persons
- Rate
- Included Services (Breakfast, taxes, etc.)
- Name and address of payee, in case it does not coincide with the guest´s name

Some hotels enforce guaranteed bookings. These are basically non-refundable bookings, where in case of a no-show, the guest agrees to pay the price of the room anyway.

At last, we should call attention to special circumstances, such as constructions, deviations, upcoming festivities, strikes or others. We thank our prospect guest for the reservation and wish them a pleasant journey.

Frequent mistakes:

- Deficient description of the hotel and offered services
- Names spelled wrong
- Omitted titles
- Arrival times or special requests not noted
- Offered value-added services cannot be provided
- No or late confirmation of the booking
- Unclear forms for online-bookings

Key to success:

- Friendliness
- Exact description of products and services
- Precise specification of prices and payment methods
- Destination instructions and information
- Special features/ advantages of the hotel
- Convey the assertion of having picked the right place Confirm having chosen the right place

03. Arrival

Our guests will be observing the surroundings of the hotel before arriving at the actual hotel. They will expect helpful guiding (signs) towards the hotel, an free driveway and enough space to unload the car. Furthermore they will pay attention to the façade, lighted advertising, colours and the entrance. The guest will want to be greeted immediately (by their name) and helped unloading their baggage. An additional service can be to pay the taxi the guests have arrived in and charge this to their room, rather than to having the guest pay the taxi driver in an already stressful situation.

Frequent mistakes:

- Blocked driveways
- Unkempt facades
- Small or unlit signs
- Untrained staff
- Uncovered entrance (from rain, snow, sun, etc.)
- No or not enough umbrellas to protect the guests and employees

Key to success:

- Welcome Drink
- Friendly and helpful welcome -and staff
- Correct description for arrival
- Know regulars and greet them with their names
- Good first impression: make the guest feel he made the right choice by coming to this hotel
- Warm greeting

04. Check-in

Guests should be welcomed immediately after arriving and be asked whether they had a good journey. Ideally the guest will be addressed with his name. For those who already made reservations, a filled out registration form will be waiting. The guests will only have to verify their personal information and sign. Those who do not have a reservation will be assisted while filling in the form. The receptionist will fully focus on her/his present guests without any distractions. She/he will also inform the guests about their services. At last, the receptionist will wish the guests a pleasant stay. The number of the hotel room will only be disclosed to the guests and the bell boy.

Frequently made mistakes:

- Unfriendly greeting (without a smile)
- Regulars are not addressed by their names
- No assistance while filling in the registration form
- Guests are not being informed about services and special offers
- Room numbers are hearable or disclosed for everyone
- Bell boy is not being called to help with baggage
- Staff forgets to wish the guest a pleasant stay

Key to success:

- Address guests by their names and show enthusiasm
- Ask the guests, whether they had a pleasant journey
- Correctly filled in registration forms ready to sign
- Assistance to walk-ins while filling in the registration form
- Give information about services offered at the hotel
- Help with the baggage
- Accompany guests to the room

05. Hotel room

The hotel bell boy is supposed to open the door for the guest and leave the key card in the card holder in the room, turn on the lights and let the guest enter the room first. He then brings the baggage into the room and leaves it on the baggage stand. After this the bell boy opens the curtains and depending on the season and weather he opens or inclines the window. He continues by explaining the electronic appliances to the guest (such as TV, radio, AC, etc.). Showing the guest the minibar's content and its pricelist is another responsibility of the bell boy. At the end he shows the guest the bathroom and explains its appliances. He wishes the guest a pleasant stay, describes further services offered by the hotel and shows them the plan of escape in case of an emergency.

Often made mistakes:

- Outdated TV program
- Stale air or previous guest's odour is still in the air
- Burned-out light bulbs
- Expired products in the mini bar
- Non-harmonic colours
- Pressure marks from last guest on note pad
- Dusty door or picture frames
- Bell boy enters the room first
- Incomplete hotel directory, service brochure or pricelists
- Too many or too big furniture pieces
- Insufficient clothes hangers

Key to success:

- Complete cleanliness and safety
- Walk.in closet or well lit closet
- Welcome card, fresh flowers or fruits, refreshing drink on the house
- Windows that can be opened or inclined
- Appliances that are easy to operate
- Well lit room
- Phone call from reception (about 20 minutes after arrival) to make sure everything is to the guest´s satisfaction
- Safety instructions

06. Bathroom

The bathroom in the hotel room and the hotel room itself must be perfectly clean. These extras have to be found in the bathroom: soap, shampoo, body wash and sanitary bags. This depends on the category of the hotel.

There has to be an appropriate number of hand and shower-towels. They have to be soft and have an adequate size (big enough). The guest will appreciate storage surface, a lit and moveable cosmetic mirror, face wipes, bathrobes, slippers, shoe cleaning wipes, a shoehorn and a sealed toilet paper roll. The bathroom has to be equipped with an efficient and muted air condition/ exhauster, so it does not keep any humidity.

Frequent mistakes:

- Poor lighting
- Humidity or detergent smell
- Dripping taps
- Low-quality accessories
- Too small or coarse towels
- Too strong hairdryers
- humidity condensing on mirrors
- Slippery floor

Key to success:

- Bidet
- Soft and big towels
- Muted air condition / exhaustion
- Separate toilet room and shower
- Perfectly clean and safe (non-slippery floor, easy to operate appliances, rounded edges, well isolated plugs, etc.)
- Sufficient room and storage surface
- Separate bath tub and shower

07. Public rooms

Public rooms are accessible to hotel guests and daily and regular visitors as well. These are the lobby, the lounge, lifts, restaurants, bars, convention rooms, library, casino, spa, gardens, fitness studio, public restrooms, etc.

The public rooms have to be clean at all times. Well placed and lit signs will show the way.

Mistakes:

- Confusing signs
- Inconvenient location
- Neglected cleanliness
- Lacking safety
- Unfit decoration
- Insufficient lighting

Key to success:

- Well-spaced
- Comfortable and cosy seating areas
- Limited public access
- Matching atmosphere to the hotel
- Subtle decoration
- Exclusivity
- Access to bar or restaurant service
- Wi-Fi free of charge
- Background music
- Access to nationwide / international newspapers and magazines

08.   Services

The offered services depend on the category of the hotel, so a guest will expect more service from a first-class hotel than from another. A five star hotel will offer personnel to help with the baggage, valet parking, event bookings, car rentals, currency exchange, translators, dry-cleaning, room service, lost & found, message-transfer, shoe-cleaning, wake-up calls, tour- and travel bookings, PC-Butler, babysitters and a doctor. These services should be mentioned along with their respective prices and opening hours in the hotel directory.

Frequent mistakes:

- Outdated pricelists
- Changed opening hours
- Offered services, that are not provided (due to cost cuts or others)
- Confusing descriptions of services

Key to success:

- Turn Down-Service
- Event booking
- Appropriate value-for-money ratio
- Professional services
- Added value making the stay at the hotel more attractive
- Bike rentals
- Services free of charge (shoe cleaning, shuttle service, etc.)

09. Check-Out

When the guest is leaving, reception sends a bell boy to pick up the baggage. Then the mini bar will be checked, in order to charge for consumed products. The cashier or receptionist will prepare the bill in the meantime. When handing it to the guest, the receptionist will explain each position on the bill. If the guest has a complaint, she/ he will be asked into the office or away from the reception. This will be handled with discretion and if possible in favour of the guest. The "4:16 rule" has to be remembered here. A satisfied guest will spread the word four times, whereas an unsatisfied guest will do 16 times.

Frequent mistakes:

- Bill is not ready when the guest wants to check out
- The bill is closed before considering the consumption of the minibar
- The deposit is not subtracted from the total
- The guests have to wait for their baggage
- The check-out is completed but the receptionist forgets to order the bell boy to take the baggage to the taxi/car
- After checkout nobody checks the room for forgotten items.
- Baggage Mixed up

Key to success:

- Correct and structured bill
- Option of express check-out
- Friendly personnel, who assists and helps even after paying the bill
- Forwarding (shipping or mailing) of forgotten items or messages received after the guest has left the hotel

10. Staff

All personnel should be friendly, honest, attentive, flexible, confident and have a positive attitude towards the guest. They should constantly offer their services, think ahead, smile and ideally be charismatic. Body language and outfit are exemplary. The perfect employee embodies the hotels motto of always doing more and unexpected to spoil the guest.

Frequent mistakes:

- Disinterested, arrogant and/or bored staff
- Ironic, undedicated and inflexible personnel
- Employees do not take over responsibilities
- Non-enthusiastic personnel, who do not identify themselves with the spirit of the hotel and its staff
- Unmotivated staff

Key to success:

- Attentive, correct and quick assistance
- Focus on one guest at a time
- Complete and correct help
- Polite and honest behaviour towards the guest
- Competent staff
- Anticipate guests requirements and think ahead
- Understand and tolerate the guest´s needs

Checklist service-quality:

This checklist will be of use for quality checks in your own hotel or restaurant, your competitors´ hotel or restaurant, or for mystery guests and customers.

The list contains over a hundred criteria for quality, which are subcategorized into ten groups. The groups correspond to the previous sections in this book. The main criteria will be evaluated, whereas the sub criteria can serve as a memory aid. Please do not hesitate to write down your comments, as these will be useful when evaluating the list.

After testing the individual processes and departments of the facility a review will be conducted.

Excellent services will be rewarded with ten points, good ones with 7 or 8, averaged levelled services with 5 or 6, services evaluated as poor will obtain a score of 3 or 4 and bad service will obtain a score of 1 or 2. The total will give you an overall indicator of performance.

Please find the checklist comprising 10 groups with about 100 criteria as table on the following pages.

Evaluation	Valuation of quality	Hotel/Restaurant:
	☐ Outstanding: 100-91	
	☐ Excellent: 90-81	
	☐ Good: 80-71	Date:
	☐ Average: 70-61	
	☐ Poor: 60-51	
	☐ Insufficient: 50-00	

Checklist for hotels

#	Criteria	Score and comments				
01.	**First contact**	10 / 9	8 / 7	6 / 5	4 / 3	2/ 1
1.	Phone rings (3-5)					
2.	Politeness					
3.	Language					
4.	Name of the guest					
5.	Information about the hotel					
6.	Website					
7.	Advertising material					
02.	**Reservations**	10 / 9	8 / 7	6 / 5	4 / 3	2/ 1
8.	Arrival and departure, number and name of persons arriving and departing					
9.	Room type and rate					
10.	Name of cardholder					
11.	Written confirmation					
12.	Description of offered services					
13.	Efficiency / professionalism					
14.	Special circumstances (construction, etc.)					
15.	Thank you, wish a pleasant and safe trip					
03.	**Arrival**	10 / 9	8 / 7	6 / 5	4 / 3	2/ 1
16.	Directions					
17.	Signage					
18.	Drive way, parking lot or garage					
19.	Hotel advertisement on the road					
20.	Facade					
21.	Welcoming, greeting					
22.	Entrance					
23.	Baggage					
04.	**Check-In**	10 / 9	8 / 7	6 / 5	4 / 3	2/ 1
24.	Friendly greeting					
25.	Language					
26.	Confirmation of room type					
27.	Conditions of payment					
28.	Registration form					
29.	Individual care					
30.	Mail / Information					

31.	Services					
32.	Welcome drink					
33.	Handing over of keys					
34.	Phone call to confirm satisfaction with the room and service					
05.	**Hotel room**	10 / 9	8 / 7	6 / 5	4 / 3	2/ 1
35.	Baggage					
36.	Access and signage					
37.	Opening the door					
38.	Baggage stand					
39.	Instructions					
40.	Description of services					
41.	Exit of bell boy (subtly)					
42.	Air condition and temperature					
43.	Lighting					
44.	Cleanliness					
45.	Room size					
46.	Decoration and colours					
47.	Furniture					
48.	Bed and bedding					
49.	Minibar					
50.	Safe					
51.	TV/TV-Programme, Radio					
52.	Phone/Fax/Answering machine./ internet access					
53.	Hotel directory					
54.	Safety					
55.	Informative material					
56.	Welcome card or fruit basket					
57.	(Electric) clothes hanger					
58.	Noise damping					
06.	**Hotel bathroom**	10 / 9	8 / 7	6 / 5	4 / 3	2/ 1
59.	Cleanliness					
60.	Size					
61.	Air condition / exhaustion					
62.	Mirrors					
63.	Hand wash basin					
64.	Tub					
65.	Shower					
66.	WC					
67.	Accessories					
68.	Hand and shower towels					
69.	Safety					
07.	**Public rooms**	10 / 9	8 / 7	6 / 5	4 / 3	2/ 1

70.	Signage					
71.	Atmosphere					
72.	Location					
73.	Appropriate furnishing					
74.	Odours					
75.	Lighting					
76.	Decoration					
77.	Background music					
78.	Cleanliness					
08.	**Services**	10 / 9	8 / 7	6 / 5	4 / 3	2/ 1
79.	Garage/Parking lot					
80.	Concierge/porter/doorman					
81.	Room service					
82.	Dry cleaning					
83.	Convention centre					
84.	Banquet/Catering					
85.	Wellness					
86.	Restaurant, Bar etc.					
09.	**Check-out**	10 / 9	8 / 7	6 / 5	4 / 3	2/ 1
87.	Baggage					
88.	Billing					
89.	Complaint management					
90.	Waiting time					
91.	Currency exchange					
92.	Credit cards					
93.	Assistance					
94.	Thank you, pleasant and safe journey					
10.	**Staff**	10 / 9	8 / 7	6 / 5	4 / 3	2/ 1
95.	Politeness					
96.	Candidness					
97.	Attentiveness					
98.	Helpfulness					
99.	Charisma					
100.	Impeccable outfit					
101.	Appropriate body language					
102.	Languages					
103.	Pronunciation					
104.	Eagerness to learn					
	Total					
	Valuation of quality ☐　Outstanding: 100-91 ☐　Excellent: 90-81 ☐　Good: 80-71 ☐　Average: 70-61 ☐　Poor: 60-51 ☐　Insufficient: 50-00	Hotel: Date:				

Hotel guest questionnaire

Summed up in ten questions with ten evaluation points

Our criteria for quality	Your evaluation
First contact:	
Reservation: Was the booking process professional? Was the booking department attentive to every single detail? Were you well-advised, treated with respect and politely?	
Arrival: Were the directions helpful? Is the hotel well signposted? Enough parking space? Are façade and entrance well kept? Were you welcomed and helped with your luggage?	
Check-in: Did the staff give you a warm and friendly welcome? Were you assisted when filling out the registration form?	
Hotel room: How did you like your room? Was it clean? Did you like bed and bedding, size, furnishing, decoration, colours, lighting, safety and noise damping?	
Bathroom: Please assess the bathroom of your room? Consider safety, cleanliness, size, air exhaustion, towels, accessories, shower, WC, mirrors, tub, etc.	
Public rooms: How did you like the public rooms? The atmosphere, location, furnishing, lighting, decoration, etc.?	
Services:	
Staff: Was our staff polite, attentive, candid, competent and impeccably dressed?	
Check-out: Was your check-out trouble-free? Did you receive your baggage, a correct bill, assistance? In case of complaints, how would you evaluate the complaint-management?	
Total Score: (to be filled out by hotel)	

Comments:

City/Date:

Name (optional):	Address (optional):

Thank you for helping to improve our service quality!

Service quality from the restaurant guest´s view

This chapter describes the process of guest care including the services of the restaurant. After a brief description of best practices, follows a description of frequently made mistakes and the key to success.

01. First contact

01.01. Phone call, website, advertising material

The first contact with the restaurant is decisive and will leave permanent impressions, which will be hard to change. This contact can be in form of a phone call, the website or through friends´ and family members' recommendation.

In case of a call, the guest is expecting the phone to be answered quickly and friendly in their language (answer including name of the restaurant and person answering the phone, greeting, a thank you and a short introductory question). The person answering will listen to the guest´s needs and then answer, instead of shooting with information. Because business people usually are in a hurry and want to get precise information and private persons usually have more time.

The guest expects a website to be loaded in seven seconds or less and they want it to be clearly structured. The guest should be able to return to the home page from every page of the website.

The effect of a first contact is often underestimated, which is a big mistake!

Frequent mistakes:

- Answering machine
- Holding line
- Let the phone ring more than five times
- Technical language
- Uninformed beginners on the line
- Too much unnecessary information on websites and advertising
- Unfriendly staff on the line

Key to success:

- Attractive advertising, to meet potential guest´s interest
- Answering the phone not later than at the third ring
- Friendly and appropriate welcome
- Quickly loading and well-structured website

01.02. Reserving a table

In order to professionalize the whole reservation process, the guests should be addressed by their names and the offered service (e.g. menu) must comply one hundred percent with the wishes and needs the guests expressed.

If the desired service is not available, two alternatives have to be offered by explaining the differences to the service expected by the guest.

The guest´s personal information will be handled carefully, and depending on the situation a written confirmation will be offered to the guest. This will be confirmed orally before hanging up the phone:

- Name of the guest
- Date and time
- Occasion of the meal
- Number of persons
- Price
- Included services
- Name and address of payee, in case it does not coincide with the guest´s name

At last we should call attention to special circumstances, such as constructions, deviations, upcoming festivities, strikes or others. We thank our prospect guest for the reservation and wish them a nice day.

Frequent mistakes:

- Unclear forms for online-bookings
- Wrong spelled names
- Omitted titles
- No or late confirmation of the reservation
- Deficient description of the menu and offered services
- Not noted arrival times or special requests
- Offered value-added services that cannot be provided or are forgotten

Key to success:

- Special features/ advantages of the restaurant/ hotel
- Exact description of products and services
- Friendliness
- Precise specification of prices and payment methods
- Arrival description and information
- Confirm that the guest has chosen the right place

01.03. Arrival

Our guests will be observing the surroundings of the restaurant before arriving. They will expect helpful and attractive signage, an free driveway and enough parking space. Furthermore they will pay attention to the façade, lighted advertising, colours and the entrance and especially the layout of the menu. The guests want to be welcomed immediately (by their name if possible), have the door opened for them and be seated appropriately.

Frequent mistakes:

- Blocked parking lots (often by employees cars)
- No or no friendly welcome
- Uncovered entrance (from rain, snow, sun, etc.)
- No record of the reservation or no table available, though a reservation was made
- No menu or unlit menu at the entrance
- Unkempt facades
- Small or unlit signs

Key to success:

- Friendly and helpful staff
- Correct description for arrival
- Know regulars and greet them with their names
- Good first impression: make the guest feel he made the right choice by coming to this restaurant
- Welcome drink

02. Guest area

The entrance door should be signposted and easy to handle (not too heavy). The atmosphere should be positive. Smells, lighting, colours, music or noises and temperature will influence the guest´s impression of the restaurant. Important factors are the spacing and positioning of chairs and tables, dividing walls, plants and other accessories, as well.

Frequent mistakes:

- Staled air
- Positioning of furniture
- Narrow rooms
- Bad lighting
- Bad signage of doors
- Inappropriate colours
- Music too loud or noises from the kitchen

Key to success:

- Appropriate lighting and music volume
- Opening the door for our guests or automatic doors
- Wi-Fi free of charge
- Thorough ventilated rooms, appropriate temperature and no odours
- Harmonic colours
- No noise
- Well signposted emergency exits

03. Table

To make the guests feel comfortable at their table, the height of table and chairs is decisive. The size of the table and the distance to the next table or the wall, influence the comfortable feeling as well. Consider about 80 to 120cm for each guest at the table and about 100cm from the end of the table to the wall, whereas about 150cm from one table to another. It is most important, that chairs and tables do not wobble.

Frequent mistakes:

*   Narrow spaced and wobbling tables
*   Uncomfortable seats

Key to success:

*   Appropriate table-size and distance to the next guest at the table
*   Ergonomic seats

04. Mise-en-place

Mise-en-place includes preparation in the kitchen and well-trained service staff. We will focus on the staff and their duties, such as setting the tables, preparing side tables, cutlery and others.

Each section in a restaurant should have a side table ready for use, storing extra table cloths, napkins and cutlery, salt and pepper stands, ash trays and food and beverage menus.

The table should be set as following:

Cover the table with a molleton and a clean table cloth, optionally a table runner over the table cloth (protects the table cloth from stains).

Place basic tableware (knife, fork and napkin), additional tableware (plus spoon and universal glass), advanced tableware (additional plate, glass and center knife) or the complete tableware (adding cutlery for appetizers, dessert, etc.). The table will be decorated to perfection, when adding salt and pepper stands and a center piece.

Every restaurant has its own style but the tableware and decoration should be practical, helpful to the guest and in accordance with the restaurant´s style. Most important, every utensil on the table must be impeccably clean!

Frequent mistakes:

- Inconsistent setting of tables
- Insufficient extra cutlery, table cloths and/or other utensils
- Water stains on cutlery and glasses
- Stained and/ or damaged table cloths
- Sticky utensils (e.g. salt and pepper shaker)
- Too small or bad quality napkins
- Unsuitable cutlery (too small/ big)

Key to success:

- Impeccable tableware
- Suitable cutlery
- Professional advice for the use of cutlery in case of unusual dishes ordered

05. Menus

Menus should conform with the style of the restaurant and trigger the guest´s appetite. They should be well structured, easy to understand and above all be informative. The service-staff has to complement the information on the menu with competent advice.

Order of dishes in the menu (classical form):

- Appetizers, cold and warm
- Soups
- Fish
- Egg dishes
- Roasted and grilled dishes
- Game and poultry dishes
- Vegetables and salads
- Desserts
- Cheese and fruits
- Specialties of the house, dish of the day, Kids´ menu and menu for seniors, cold dishes should be emphasized, e.g. at the beginning of the menu

Frequent mistakes:

- Stained or dirty menus
- Wrong prices
- Insufficient number of menus
- Text too small
- Technical language
- Fantasy names without description

Key to success:

- Well-structured menus, that are easy to understand
- All dishes displayed can be served
- Interesting food and beverage menus

06. Service

Even though the service has to be as professional as possible, a candid and warm service is important too. Our guests are kings and queens and each one deserves an individual service.

Proper service includes:

Warm greeting, seating, handing over the menus following protocol, taking beverage orders and serving, informing about menu and assisting with selection, serving dishes following protocol, anticipate guest´s needs, clearing the table, offering dessert or digestive drink and serving these, billing, see guests off and thank them for their visit.

Frequent mistakes:

- Guests seat themselves and have to wait for somebody to notice them
- No welcoming
- Physical contact with the guest
- Deficient assistance of the staff
- Impersonal or too personal service
- Unfriendly tone during the restaurant service
- Mix-up of dishes

Key to success:

- Attentive, friendly, polite and helpful staff and service
- Good assistance
- Clear and comprehensible way of speaking
- Individual treatment while staying factual
- Quick service
- Immediate welcome
- Competent and honest assistance
- Listen to the guest and be patient

07. Food / Meals

Quantity and quality should comply with the guest´s expectations a hundred percent. Importance of the appearance of the dish, combination of colours, texture, smell, proportions, garnish and the salad should not be neglected.

As important as the quality of the food, is the presentation on the plate. Warm meals should be served on preheated plates, whereas cold dishes do not necessarily require a pre-cooled plate.

Frequent mistakes:

- Classy but small portion
- Food from can
- Big plates, but small portions
- Mush instead of sauce
- Fish taste is too strong
- Indeterminable stodge
- A lot on the plate, but nothing that stands out
- Warm dish served cold on hot plate
- Stringy food

Key to success:

- Guest wants to come back
- Guest asks for the recipe
- Guest wants to complement the chef
- Guest orders the same as last time, or guest´s companion orders the same
- Food tastes homemade
- - Guests are well advised
- Guest recommends the restaurant

08. Beverages

As for food, quality and quantity play an important role with beverages.

Refreshing drinks, such as Cola or lemonade, should indeed be refreshing. Therefore they should be cool, fresh and sparkling.

Beer should be served cold as well, with a head and the glass should mist up.

White wine has to be served cool and should not be let standing to breathe, as it is the case with red wine.

Sparkling wine cannot lose the sparkling effect and has to be served cooled.

Beverages served from the bar have to be served in gauged glasses or steins.

Frequent mistakes:

- Stale beer
- Half-filled glasses
- Lacking gas in refreshing beverages
- Watery coffee
- Hot drinks served cold and vice versa

Key to success:

- Good wine selection
- Freshly squeezed orange juice
- Guest wants to come back
- Guest repeats order

09. Staff

All personnel should be friendly, honest, attentive, flexible, confident and have a positive attitude towards the guest. They should constantly offer their services, think ahead, smile and ideally be charismatic. Body language and outfit are exemplary. The perfect employee embodies the hotel's motto of always doing more and unexpected to spoil the guest.

Frequent mistakes:

- Disinterested, arrogant and/or bored staff
- Ironic, undedicated and inflexible personnel
- Employees who do take over responsibilities
- Non-enthusiastic personnel, who does not identify themselves with the spirit of the hotel and its staff
- Unmotivated staff

Key to success:

- Attentive, correct and quick assistance
- Focus on one guest at a time
- Complete and correct advice on services and products
- Polite and honest behaviour towards the guest
- Competent staff
- Anticipate guest´s requirements and think ahead
- Understand and tolerate the guest´s needs

Value-for-money

The value-for-money is a very difficult factor to evaluate, as it depends on multiple criteria:

- Guest´s disposition (guests in a jovial mood, are more willing to pay a higher price)
- Current financial situation of the guest
- Price checks
- Level of guest's experience with restaurants
- Wishes and expectations of the guest

Checklist Service-quality

This checklist will be of use for quality checks in your own restaurant, your competitors´ hotel or restaurant, or for mystery guests and customers.

The list contains over a hundred criteria for quality, which are subcategorized into ten groups. The groups correspond to the previous sections in this book. The main criteria will be evaluated, whereas the sub-criteria can serve as a memory aid. Please do not hesitate to write down your comments, as these will be useful for evaluating the list.

After testing the individual processes and departments of the facility an review will be conducted.

Excellent services will be rewarded with ten points, good ones with 7 or 8, averaged levelled services with 5 or 6, services evaluated as poor will obtain a score of 3 or 4 and bad service will obtain a score of 1 or 2. The total will give you an overall indicator of performance.

Please find the checklist comprising 10 groups with about 100 criteria as table on the following pages

Evaluation	Valuation of quality	Hotel/Restaurant:
	☐ Outstanding: 100-91	
	☐ Excellent: 90-81	
	☐ Good: 80-71	Date:
	☐ Average: 70-61	
	☐ Poor: 60-51	
	☐ Insufficient: 50-00	

Checklist for restaurants

#	Criteria	Score and comments				
01.	**First contact**	**10 / 9**	**8 / 7**	**6 / 5**	**4 / 3**	**2/ 1**
1.	Phone rings (3-5)					
2.	Politeness					
3.	Language					
4.	Name of the guest					
5.	Information about the restaurant					
6.	Website					
7.	Advertising material					
8.	Table reservation					
9.	Signage					
10.	Drive way, parking lot or garage					
11.	Facade					
02.	**Guest area**	**10 / 9**	**8 / 7**	**6 / 5**	**4 / 3**	**2/ 1**
12.	Entrance					
13.	Odours					
14.	Lighting					
15.	Colours					
16.	Noise or music					
17.	Temperature					
18.	Room layout					
19.	Furniture					
20.	Atmosphere					
21.	Other rooms					
03.	**Table**	**10 / 9**	**8 / 7**	**6 / 5**	**4 / 3**	**2/ 1**
22.	Table					
23.	Chair					
24.	Distance					
25.	Measures					
26.	Ergonometric					
27.	Style					
28.	Arrangement of furniture					
29.	Harmony					
04.	**Mise-en-place**	**10/9**	**8 / 7**	**6 / 5**	**4 / 3**	**2/ 1**
30.	Molleton					
31.	Table cloth					
32.	Table runner					
33.	Tableware					
34.	Cutlery					
35.	Glasses					
36.	Plates					

37.	Salt and pepper stands					
38.	Napkins					
39.	Storage					
40.	Side table					
41.	Extra utensils					
05.	**Menus**	**10/9**	**8 / 7**	**6 / 5**	**4 / 3**	**2/ 1**
42.	Food					
43.	Wine / Beverages					
44.	Desserts menu					
45.	Well designed					
46.	Clean					
47.	Logical structure					
48.	comprehensiveness					
49.	Correct prices					
50.	Current specials					
51.	Appetizers: warm a. cold					
52.	Soups					
53.	Fish					
54.	Egg meals					
55.	Roasted and grilled dishes					
56.	Game and poultry dishes					
57.	Desserts					
58.	Cheese and fruits					
59.	Specialty of the house					
60.	Today´s special					
61.	Kids 'menu, menu for seniors					
62.	Cold dishes (small menu)					
06.	**Service**	**10 / 9**	**8 / 7**	**6 / 5**	**4 / 3**	**2/ 1**
63.	Greeting					
64.	Seating					
65.	Handing over of menus					
66.	Taking drink orders					
67.	Serving drinks					
68.	Taking food orders					
69.	Serving food					
70.	Assisting and advising					
71.	Clearing the table					
72.	Billing					
73.	Seeing off the guest					
07.	**Food / Meals**	**10 / 9**	**8 / 7**	**6 / 5**	**4 / 3**	**2/ 1**
74.	Quality					
75.	Quantity					
76.	Presentation					
77.	Combination of colours					
78.	Texture					
79.	Smell					

80.	Meat / side dish / garnish					
81.	Sauce					
82.	Plate					
08.	**Drinks**	10 / 9	8 / 7	6 / 5	4 / 3	2/ 1
83.	Quality					
84.	Quantity					
85.	Freshness					
86.	Temperature					
87.	Suitable glasses					
88.	Sufficiency of offer					
89.	Advice on drinks					
90.	Restaurant's selection wine					
09.	**Staff**	10 / 9	8 / 7	6 / 5	4 / 3	2/ 1
91.	Politeness					
92.	Candidness					
93.	Attentiveness					
94.	Helpfulness					
95.	Charisma					
96.	Acceptable outfit					
97.	Appropriateness of body language					
98.	Languages					
99.	Pronunciation					
100.	Eagerness to learn					
10.	**Value-for-money rate**	10 / 9	8 / 7	6 / 5	4 / 3	2/ 1
101.	Appropriateness					
102.	Comparable with competitors					
103.	Accordance to local market rate					
104.	Price leading					
	Total					

Valuation of quality	Restaurant:
☐ Outstanding: 100-91	
☐ Excellent: 90-81	Date:
☐ Good: 80-71	
☐ Average: 70-61	
☐ Poor: 60-51	
☐ Insufficient: 50-00	

Restaurant guest questionnaire

Summed up in ten questions with ten evaluation points

Our criteria for quality	Your evaluation
First contact:	
Guest area: How did you like entrance, smell, temperature, lighting, decoration, colours, furnishing, room layout, atmosphere, style, etc.?	
Table: Did you find tables and chairs convenient?, (Distances, comfortable chairs , ,, style, etc.)	
Preparation: Did you find suitable table ware (cutlery, centre piece, extra utensils)?	
Menus: Are the menus clean and attractive, well-structured and are the dishes balanced? Is the display of the prices correct?	
Service: did you like the service: greeting, seating, handing over of menus, advice, taking drink and food orders correctly, serving, clearing the table, anticipation of waiters, billing, seeing off the guest?	
Food: Please assess quality, proportion, quantity, presentation , texture, taste, smell, temperature of plates	
Drinks: Please assess quality, quantity, temperature, freshness, glasses suitability, advice	
Staff: Was our staff polite, attentive, candid, competent and impeccably dressed?	
Value-for-money rate: Was it appropriate, comparable with competitors, according to the local market's rate? Was the price fair?	
Total Score: (to be filled in by restaurant)	

Comments:

City/Date:

Name (optional):	Address (optional):

Thank you for helping us improve our service quality!

Final review

These checks are designed to assess your service quality rather harsh, but to your benefit. You will be able to detect the weaknesses in your establishment, in order to conduct improvements and train your staff appropriately. Please do not hesitate to develop your own checklists and perform quality checks on a regular basis.

Your guests perceive your house and service as a unity, therefore you should focus on every little detail in order to achieve the highest quality level possible, because;

There is only one view on service quality, and that's the guest´s view!

Best Practice

Excerpt from Mr. Lucy's diary

Today, I arrived in Monteverde. The Ascot Hotel´s chauffeur picked me up from the airport and took me to the hotel. I was very surprised when I arrived there. Let me describe in detail what impressed me the most:

Transfer:

The gentleman that picked me up was already expecting me in the arrival hall with a sign with my name and the name of the hotel. Extremely noticeable was that the sign had a horse´s head´s shape, as that is the logo of the hotel. After a short ride of approximately ten minutes we arrived at the hotel, where I noticed they had renovated its façade.

At the Airport, Mr. Don Gentil, driver of the private taxi company "Remis" was waiting for me at the arrivals. I could recognize this quickly by a sticker showing the hotel's name and logo (a horse's head). It didn't take ten minutes and we arrived at the driveway. With pleasure I noted the hotel's renewed façade and new lettering. I looked forward to what I would find interesting inside.

Appearance of the hotel:

The hotel looked very well kept, since you could see it was recently painted. When I saw the front yard, I could not help myself but I notice the lovely exotic ornamental plants. Moreover, they had an inviting winter garden which I would enjoy later. The seven international flags hanging at the entrance of the hotel create a cosmopolitan flair. The bell boy was already waiting for me, as soon as we drove into the drive way. He opened the car and the hotel door as well for me greeting me with my name and immediately he took my baggage. The welcoming reception I got, made me feel incredibly comfortable with my decision of coming back to this hotel.

Reception:

When entering I was very impressed by the lobby, not because of its size, but because of its classy furnishing and decoration. The décor items all reminded me of the famous Ascot horse race track in England, which landed the hotel its name of. Besides, also the staffs´ uniforms and the complete ambience reminded me of this place where you can dream-travel into another world.

The receptionist, Mr. Polyglott, welcomed me warmly in German. He had already filled in the registration form for me, so I only had to check its correctness and sign. This saved time and allowed me to go to my room to rest immediately, as I had a 20 hour flight.

Hotel Room:

The bell boy showed me into my room which I liked at first sight, by simply activating the key card. The room had a high quality carpet, a closet with ten hangers and a safe, which was easy to handle.

I was relieved to find an anti-allergically pillow in the top shelf of the closet, next to an extra blanket. The room was spacious, so I walked all the way over to the baggage stand where the helpful bell boy had placed my suitcase. He also explained all the electrical appliances in the room to me before subtly leaving my room. The king size bed and furniture was very elegant and comfortable. Everything matched the colour of the walls. I sat down to read the TV manual, having enough reading light from the floor lamp beside me. The mini bar was well filled; the phone had an extra plug for a fax machine or an internet connection. The room even had an electrical pants hanger. All in all I was extremely satisfied with the room; I had no wishes left to fulfil and would absolutely recommend the hotel especially to business travellers.

Bathroom:

The bathroom was fully tiled, contained a bathtub with shower and a sliding separating screen. The extra bidet was nice to have, but not really necessary for me as a business traveller. The bathroom appliances were modern; therefore the shower head was moveable. I could see myself in the big crystal mirror above the wash basin, which was extremely well lit from all sides. What I appreciated most was the environmental consciousness of the hotel. They had installed shampoo and soap dispensers and a two-phased toilet flush. Guests were informed about the environmental option to keep the towels for several days.

Bar:

Mini bar prices and prices from the bar were identical, so I enjoyed a cold beer from the mini bar. After that I decided to go to the „WINNER-BAR" for a more social atmosphere. Its British décor is originally from a closed down bar from London. The bar menu was very appealing; it offered tapped beer, light and modern drinks, open premium hotel's selection wines, sparkling wines and snacks. I decided to redeem a voucher for a cocktail I received on my arrival.

Café:

The café opens at 7 a.m., where you can enjoy an extensive breakfast buffet until 11 a.m. After that you can order meals "á la minute" at reasonable prices (salads, consommés, crêpes, steaks, sandwiches, etc.) until night time. In the afternoon I enjoyed tea and cake, which I picked out of a rich selection of cakes, while looking at the beautiful view from the terrace and winter garden.

Events:

I was interested in seeing what kind of events were going on at the hotel, so I asked the concierge for some information and he showed me the event folder. It looked very appealing and therefore I was well instructed. I really liked the fact that he displayed me all events including prices.

The hotel has a conference room and a small ballroom. The conference room can accommodate about 20 to 40 people. This nice saloon has access to the garden as well to the winter garden. Whereas the ballroom accommodates 40 to 80 people, also usable for bigger conferences. The terrace or winter garden then serves for catering.

Staff:

The staff is very competent and professional. They were always attentive and eager to help with any assistance I needed. I really liked their uniforms, which reminded of the hotel´s name and logo. Besides, a waiter told me that there was a hotel school along with the hotel – as taken from a Swiss example. This might save up to 30% personnel cost.

All together I enjoyed my stay at the Ascot very much and would absolutely recommend it to my colleagues and friends.

Extra services:

- Horse riding and tennis at the Cabrasco Polo Club
- Golfing at the Punta Cabrasco Golf Club
- Sailing at Yacht Club Monteverde
- Carriage rides through Cabrasco and its surroundings

Final review:

This hotel has gone through some changes:

- Instead of Stone Cottage, which suggested mountains, cottages, continental Europe, it changed its name and image to Ascot. This name suggests superiority, prestige, horses, luck (horseshoes) and action.
- The vacant restaurant became a snappy, chic café with changing offers of food.
- Well organized events program
- Well trained staff
- Modern price policy: identical prices for single- and double-bed rooms.
- Comprehensive information material
- Guest oriented management with the ability to change customers into regular switch then become ambassadors of the hotel.

Signature: Felix Lucky

Brief description of services offered by HOTQUA

All of our service packages are complementary and assist our clients step by step in achieving a noticeably improved service quality. This will help you to strengthen your position in the market.

We start by gathering information and data about the current quality situation; we then train your staff and implement the new and individual quality management according to ISO 9001 in your house. For that purpose we employ the model quality management manual for hotels and restaurants developed by HOTQUA. It is based on the international norms of ISO 9001 and it is certified by TÜV and CERTQUA. It has also been tested and proven to be excellent in the field. It is available via internet and also in CD-format. This allows you as our clients to implement quality management without being tied to a place, time and availability of others.

So far HOTQUA has conducted over 400 workshops with

- 4.000 participants
- 1.500 companies
- 45 of them working with the quality management system and standards developed by HOTQUA.

Berlin, 16.08.2014

Our workshops for staff and management and junior employees:

Workshops

Recommendations for your personnel:

- Service-quality from the guest´s view
- Communicate successfully with the guests
- Professional at the front office
- Complaint Management (Hotel or Restaurant)
- Hygiene and Process in the Kitchen/Housekeeping

Seminars for managers

Recommendations for middle management:

- Conflict Management for department heads
- Personnel Management for supervisors of hotels/restaurants
- Management and Marketing for Hotels and Restaurants

Courses in Quality Management

Recommendations for middle and top management:

- Quality Representative ISO 9001
- Quality Manager ISO 9001
- Quality Auditor ISO 9001

Your advantages:

- o Practically orientated
- o Little time needed
- o Internalizing service mentality
- o Lively and inspiring training methods
- o Quick transfer of knowledge into practice
- o Sustainable effect on quality awareness
- o Higher level of qualification for participants

The author: Frank Höchsmann

Frank Höchsmann is a qualified business economist (German equivalent to an MBA) and certified quality auditor. He was manager of a medium-sized hotel nearby Cologne, Germany during the mid-seventies.

Until the end of the eighties he was head of the tourism department at a college in Bogotá, Colombia.

In the 1990ies Frank Höchsmann led the staff training department off the Uruguayan union of hotels and restaurants. Meanwhile he published several books in the field of hotel and tourism management.

He moved back to Germany in 2001, where he founded the consulting company called HOTQUA concerned with hotel and tourism quality, together with his wife Martha Höchsmann.

Frank Höchsmann has been member of the board of the Tourism Association Berlin Reinickendorf for several years now. He is furthermore active in the Carl-Wolff-Organization, also called the Transylvanian Saxon Business Club of Germany (registered association).